Although I have taken many w
books, this one gave me some
implement in my book marketing plan.

Carol Ann Round, author

Kathryn gives the writer place after place where they can advertise
their book for free. Free is good.

Donna J. Thompson, author

After reading this book, I realized that you don't have to spend a lot
of money to publicize your work.

Mike Nach, author

A handy reference for all authors...practical advice on how to market
your paperback or eBook at hardly any cost.

Lynda Dickson, Books Direct

Short but pithy.

Valerie W. Stasik, author

Concise, accessible and filled with specific links and concrete
suggestions for you to market your book affordably and
immediately.

Carolyn Campbell, author

I've read countless other guides to try to figure out how to market my
books, but they either gave incomplete information or they were
confusing. This short book is loaded with helpful information that
anybody can use.

Maria Miller, author

This is an extremely useful little book...jam packed with tips that will help you market your book.

Charlie Bray, author

I highly recommend this book to the new author and anyone needing a quick update on book marketing.

Michelle Renea Anderson, author

I didn't expect a lot [from this book], because there are quite a few of these books already in circulation. Most of them basically say the same thing and most of them claim that they have the secret to success contained within. Kathryn's book doesn't do that. Instead, it offers a breakdown of low-budget marketing options for authors to try in an easy-to-read format...

Matthew Keith, author

Packed with commonsense wisdom...

RKG Reviews

There are a lot of links if you're looking to market your book, but can't spend a fortune doing it.

M. Brown, author

This book provided valuable resources and new website names and contact links that I'd never heard before.

Mishael Austin Witty, author

Buy it, read it, and use it as a platform for further learning and understanding of the marketing side of the publishing business.

Stephanie Keys, author

Marketing Your Book
on a Budget

Books by Kathryn Elizabeth Jones

A River of Stones

Conquering Your Goliaths: A Parable of the Five Stones

Conquering Your Goliaths: Guidebook

Marketing Your Book on a Budget

Scrambled

The Feast: A Parable of the Ring

Marketing Your Book on a Budget

KATHRYN ELIZABETH JONES

Idea Creations Press
www.ideacreationspress.com

Idea Creations Press
www.ideacreationspress.com

ASIN: B0094XV6MA
ISBN-13: 978-0988810709
ISBN-10: 0988810700
Printed in the U.S.A.

In 2002, when my first book, *A River of Stones*, was released, I had no idea how to market it. I felt sort of like a stranger in a strange new land of author signings, reviews and book talks.

And that's just about all I did when it came to marketing.

Now, some years later, I've learned a few things. About writing, about publishing, about marketing, and I've come to the conclusion that nothing worth having comes easy, but that working hard and knowing a few secrets helps to ease the journey along the way.

I hope to not only ease your journey, but help you in making the experience positive and rewarding. I also hope you will see the true reason for marketing your book; if it's money, fine, but if you can find a deeper reason for your desire to market, then you'll find your journey that much sweeter.

This book is small for a reason. For one, I wanted you to be able to afford it. Believe me when I say I know all about the starving author.

For another, it's easy to say you're going to market your book, far more difficult to actually do it, but this handy guide will help you every step of the way, even while your heart is pumping wildly the first time you have to speak about your book to someone else.

Marketing Your Book on a Budget 2012 was a huge success. In the 2013 edition, material was updated including links. In the 2014 edition expect new chapters, places to record your own discoveries and more!

Happy marketing!

Kathryn

Contents

Reviews

Reviewers. Who are they and how do they help in selling your book?

Who are they?

Book reviewers are a little like editors and a little like book readers. They tell the public what they like and don't like about your book, may spell out some grammar problems, but usually take the approach of giving you as positive a review as possible—even if they don't particularly like your book.

You will, however, come up against reviewers who take the negative approach, so expect to get reviews not to your liking. Read the review and then move on. Don't contact the reviewer and ask a bunch of questions about why he/she wrote such a negative review. Don't write something scathing back, or feel that you must somehow get their review taken off of Amazon. Keep moving forward. There have been a few times when I've wondered if the reviewer actually read the book I'd written, and I decided to look to the reviewers who liked my book and to my heart for the truth.

Where do you look?

When looking for a book reviewer, (though reviewers span the newspaper and magazine worlds), where you're really going to gain interest is through blog reviewers. Though the first two sources will get the word out, more and more readers are turning to the Internet for answers to the question, "What is the next book I should read?"

Why not be where the readers are?

For my first book, there were few blog reviewers out there, but things have changed. When I began searching online for reviewers for my book, "Conquering Your Goliaths: A Parable of the Five Stones," I was pleasantly surprised at the growth of book bloggers.

Not only were there multiple sites available, but sites that gave me a list of reviewers, the types of books reviewed, where the reviews were posted, how long the reviewer had been blogging and what form of book they accepted (PDF, paperback only; I'll discuss this more in detail later). Time was saved in searching the Internet for individual reviewers who may or may not have been interested in my book.

Here are five ideas to get you started:

1. **Step by Step Self Publishing**
   www.Stepbystepselfpublishing.net/reviewer-list.html is a great place to start. The reviewer list is easily accessible on the site by clicking on the link on the main page, "Reviewer list."
2. **Book Reviewer Yellow Pages** is a book brought to you by the site above, but portions of the listing come to you FREE through your email. If you join the mailing list at:

www.stepbystepselfpublishing.net you'll get a monthly list of new reviewers sent directly to you.

3. **The Indie View** (www.theindieview.com/indie-reviewers/) offers an updated monthly list of new book reviewers.

4. **Wise Words-Book Blogger** (www.louisewise.com/p/authors-directory.html) gives you an authors' directory; in addition, get a list of places to market your book, book publishing services, cover designers and more.

5. **Book Review Depo** is a closed group on Facebook offering a place for authors to put the word out that they need reviewers for their book. **Review Seekers** is also a closed group on Facebook that pretty much does the same thing.

Other ways to find reviewers online include:

- Social media sites like Twitter and Facebook can help you discover new and established reviewers.
- Find a blog site that does book reviews and check out their list of favorite links. You may find more blog reviewer friends listed.
- Send an email to your writer friends. Ask them who reviewed their books. Get contact information.
- Google, "**Book Reviewers.**" See what comes up. Add your genre to get a more defined list of reviewers who review your type of book.
- Check out www.Goodreads.com. This site caters to book lovers and the books they like; get some great book reviewers here.

How to send a review query:

When sending out a request for a book review, it's just that, a request. The request needs to be short and to the point. Here's the request I used for "Conquering Your Goliaths: A Parable of the Five Stones."

Dear _____,

I'm looking for *reviewers for my second book, "Conquering your Goliaths--A Parable of the Five Stones," a fictional story (with a non-fiction twist) about a woman named Ms. Virginia Bean and her quest to gather the five stones she needs to meet her Goliath--a new job.

The book is published through CreateSpace via Amazon.com. To learn more about me and about my book please feel free to visit my website: www.ariverofstones.com. My book was released on January 22, 2012.

I look forward to hearing from you.

Sincerely,

Kathryn Jones

*I have heard recently that some reviewers hate form letters like these; they prefer you go to their website, check out what they do, and write up a personal note, but I have had great success doing it the 'form letter' way.

If you're concerned about your request being a bit impersonal, add a line or two directly to the reviewer.

In the long run, however, consider how much you have on your plate; simplicity is really the key to getting the book reviews you need.

Social media groups can help. There are many directed to just such a thing: *getting the reviewers you want.* I have seen review groups on Facebook and LinkedIn, and use them every time I have a new book released.

Book Request Tips:

- When sending off a manuscript to a reviewer, don't use fancy type, use the bloggers first name, and make sure you keep things brief. As you can see, I included: name of book, book genre, short blurb about the book, where the book is published, my website where the blogger can see more of my work, and the book's release date.
- Many bloggers will accept PDF versions of your book for their Kindle or Nook. If they want a paperback copy, send it, but if they are able to read your book in a PDF format, so much the better. You personally save on the cost of your book and the postage in getting it to them. Many sites that cater to book reviews will list how they will accept a book. If you only want to send to reviewers who will review from a Kindle, for example, you can easily remove reviewers from your list that will only accept a paperback version.
- Afraid of a negative review? Don't be. Again, you'll probably get at least one. Not everyone who reviews your book is going to like it, but that doesn't mean your book isn't well written. Reviewers will give you between 1 and 5 stars, (or some other similar form of rating number) and this rating may be on their website or other websites they decide to post

their reviews such as: GoodReads, Amazon or Barnes & Noble. Remember: Negative reviews sell books too.

- If you decide to invite friends or acquaintances to review your book ask them how they would pitch your book to libraries, book stores or readers. Much of what I do with "Conquering Your Goliaths: A Parable of the Five Stones" in regards to marketing came from friends who loved my book. Use this pitch when asking for assistance.

- Ask for an endorsement. Endorsements can be placed on your website/blog or inside your book.

- One more thing! You never, ever have to pay for a review (nor should you). There are plenty of reviewers out there happy to review your book without payment. One wonders anyway, if paying for a review, how honest it will be!

A few reviewers I have used: (Keep in mind that I write Christian fiction, nonfiction and cozy mystery, but some of these reviewers review more than one genre).

- **Books Direct Books Direct** (www.booksdirect.wordpress.com)
- **Broken Teepee** (www.brokenteepee.com/)
- **Carol Round** (carolaround.com/)
- **Celtic Lady's Reviews** with Kathleen Kelly (celticladysreviews.blogspot.com/)
- **Cozy Mystery Book Reviews** (cozymysterybookreviews.com/)
- **Emeraldfire's Bookmark** with Mareena McGirr (rubyandthetwins.blogspot.com)
- **It's All About Me** (www.heathercim.wordpress.com)
- **Joan's Musings** (wwwjoansmusings.blogspot.com/)

- **Marsha L. Randolph** (marsharandolph.wordpress.com)
- **One Desert Rose** (www.onedesertrose.blogspot.com)
- **Reader's Favorite** (readersfavorite.com/)
- **Ro-Always Inspired** with Roberta Goodman (www.rogoodman.com/)
- **Shayna Gier** (shaynagier.com)
- **Sheila Deeth Blog** (sheiladeeth.blogspot.com/)
- **W.A. Thurston** (www.edwardhilarybumble.com)
- **Wall-to-Wall Books** (wall-to-wall-books.blogspot.com/)

In the long run, reviews are probably the most powerful way to get your name out there. But you must be willing to take the criticism as well as the praise.

You can also become a book reviewer. I do an occasional book review on my blog at: (www.ariverofstones.com) and receive double to triple the visits whenever I do. Book Sneeze (www.booksneeze.com) is a good place to start as a reviewer, especially if you don't have your own blog set up yet. You can also be reviewer on Amazon.

Have you ever **traded a review?** Check out the current star rating of the reviewer (1-5 stars on Amazon; I never swap with someone getting all low ratings; 1-2 stars) you'd like to exchange with and mention that you'd like to swap. (You can often find writers who want to swap reviews on social media sites or on their blog).

I usually swap with authors who have written a book similar to my own (yes, competition is helpful) or I swap with an author whose book genre is one I usually read.

Some writers believe that swapping interviews is not impartial, but I have found that, when I do my homework, the swap is beneficial to both parties. But you need to be honest with your review. If you feel as if the book you're reading is a 3 star book, and your swapping partner feels like your book is a 4, don't be afraid to be honest about your review, even though he/she rated you higher.

Obviously, not everyone is comfortable swapping reviews, but if you know that you can be honest (no matter the outcome) swapping reviews is a great way to get the reviews you need.

Book Club Reviews

Something I am just beginning to tap into. The basic jest of it is this:

Your book is included in the book club list if you also purchase other book club books that you personally review. **4 Writers and Readers** (ravereviewsbynonniejules.wordpress.com/book-club-selections-for-review) does this sort of exchange, and allows you to get honest reviews of your book in exchange for honest reviews that you give other writers.

Your Findings

Your Findings

Kathryn Elizabeth Jones

Your Findings

Interviews

Interviews are of four types:
> **Blog Interviews**
> **Radio Interviews**
> **Television Interviews**

Let's talk about each one individually.

Blog Interviews

A blog interview is one where the blog owner interviews you on their site via a questionnaire. Once they decide that you'd make a great interviewee, (they decide this based on book topic, experience, or maybe even a hole they need to fill on their blog) you're sent a form where you fill out the answers to their questions.

Questions range from, "How did you come to write your book?" to "What do you hope your readers will learn from your book?" Topics include how you best use your writing time, what you do when you have writer's block, etc.

The great thing about a blog interview is that you don't need to worry about messing up. You can write down your answers, edit for better flow, and turn them in to the blog owner in just the way you would wish to answer during an interview. The blog owner lets you know the day the interview will be posted, and once it is, you are able to let your friends and family members know about the interview via social media sites like Twitter and Facebook.

Some sites where I've done blog interviews:

- **4 Writers and Readers** (4writersandreaders.com/)
- **The Book Snoop** (www.thebooksnoop.com/)
- **Dayna Leigh Cheser** (daynalcheser.com/)
- **Deanie blog** (deanieblog.wordpress.com/)
- **Digital Book Today.com** (digitalbooktoday.com/)
- **Guiltless Reading** (guiltlessreading.blogspot.com)
- **I Am a Reader Not a Writer** (www.iamareader.com)
- **Kindle Mojo** (www.kindlemojo.com) provides author interviews and links
- **Lisa Haselton's Reviews and Interviews** (lisahaseltonsreviewsand**interviews**.blogspot.com/)
- **Matthew Keith** (matthewkeithreviews.blogspot.com/)
- **MorgenBailey'sWritingBlog** (morgenbailey.wordpress.com) I can't say enough about Morgen's blog. It is a must for marketing!
- **Welcome to the ToiBox** (etoithomas.com)

Radio Interviews

A step up from a blog interview is a radio interview, whether it's through your local station or through an online radio source like Author Talk (www.toginet.com). A radio interview spreads the word, but it is a bit harder to get than a blog interview. The good news is that if you already have a few reviews in place, and a few blog interviews, you'll have a good foundation for a radio host to take an interest in you and your work.

On toginet.com, for example, you can scroll through a list of radio show personalities and the genre of books they cover. If they're interested in your topic, you receive a list of possible questions the host will cover. You may even be given an opportunity to add questions to the list that reflect your book.

Some radio interviewers will even do a book review as part of their show, allowing even more exposure for your book and those who are listening in.

Radio Tips:

- You don't need to pay for a radio interview to be interviewed. A few stations charge, but there are plenty of free opportunities out there such as **Dawn Tevy's Blog Talk Radio show** at (blogtalkradio.com/angelsandwarriors) so don't fork out the wad unless you feel like it's a good investment. You can also start your own Blog Talk Radio show by clicking the red button at the top of the screen.

- **The Author's Show** (www.wnbnetworkwest.com/WnbAuthorsShow.html) or one of its subsidiaries such as The Christian Authors Show provides free radio interviews. Some paid features as well. You may also want to try: Book Report Radio (www.bookreportradio.com). Contact Elaine at: elaine@bookreportradio.com.

Additional Tips Include:

- Don't write down the answers to the questions the host gives you before the interview. It's a good idea to go through the questions that will be asked of you, but quite another to read them as answers. Shows want you to be natural in your responses.
- During the interview, be honest. Try to relax. This isn't always easy, so tell yourself you're just talking to a friend.
- Blog radio interviews will be easier to get than local radio station interviews, so focus your attention on what works. As you become well-known as an author, local radio stations will gladly pick you up.
- Look for folks who are just beginning their radio stint and are hungry for interviewee's.
- Join writer oriented social networking groups and keep tabs on those who ask for authors to interview.
- Selling tons of copies of your book after the program shouldn't be as important as helping fulfill the needs of your readers. One radio program I was on wanted to know about my book, *Scrambled*. I brought out that although it was fiction, the main character, Susan, goes through much of what women go through when trying to decide whether to remain with their husband or leave him.
- Make your book relevant to the lives of your readers and you will gain interest and possibly some new sales.

What I've learned about writing a book is that you won't please everyone. The good news is that, especially with my marketing book where yearly updates are the rule, I can always improve upon what is currently working for writers and make the next one better. Something we all want.

Television Interviews:

- Let's be honest, television interviews are nigh to impossible to get as a new author, that is, unless you know someone in the industry. A better idea is to get your radio interviews going and be prepared for a television host to see what successful book promotion you've already done and the interest you've already gleaned.
- Some cities have short television spots; say 15 minutes, where you can promote your work. These spots usually run mid-day around the time of the newscast; but again, it's tough to get on these shows unless you are fairly well-known or know someone in the industry.

Your Findings

Kathryn Elizabeth Jones

Your Findings

Blogs: Yours & Others

Do you have your own website? Do you blog?

Blogs are a great way to command an audience and bring new readers to you. Make your website a blog or embed your blog in your website. There are several great blogging sites on the Internet, the two biggest are: www.blogger.com – Use your Google account to access.

www.wordpress.com – Lots of free templates.

When it comes to offering an engaging author's website, there are as many opinions as there are flavors of ice-cream. Still, in the midst of mint chocolate and vanilla bean there are some standards that can't be missed.

White space: Less is more, and the more white space you have around your website's text the better. Shorten sentences, take out words that really don't need to be there; in a nutshell, consider the time factor. How long will it take the casual visitor to read over your main page? If it's more than a couple of minutes, reconsider the text.

Make it easy to read: Don't use fancy text, and watch the background color. Make the text easy on the eyes. For tips, check

out the ideas at:
www.zenfulcreations.com/resources/design/web_best_colors.htm.

Correct typos: Keep your site professional. You are a writer after all. If you put out a blog post and discover later that it has a typo or two, return immediately and correct it. Better yet, get another set of eyes to read over the document before posting it.

Articles: Make them short, no more than 500-700 words. If readers have to scroll down to read the story they might not finish it.

Use video as much as possible: Video placed at the top of your first page does wonders for traffic. Consider putting yourself on 'film' using social media sites like YouTube. What reader won't view a short clip about your book over having to read about it? Some writers read the first chapter of their new book on video, while others focus on a teaser that shows off their new book with text and music.

Let your readers see you: Place a picture of yourself on the front page. While still keeping your site professional, let your readers know who you are.

Make your pages easy to maneuver: There is nothing worse than not being able to find a particular book because of the seemingly limitless tabs. Narrow down the options to five or less and make it easy for visitors to enjoy your site. Make it easy for them to order or to email you if they have questions. And answer these questions promptly. Make the links easy to find, bolded and not hidden away in some corner.

Let social media friends know when a new story or blog is posted: Make sure they get the direct links; repost the blog posts that have been getting the most hits (for those who may have missed seeing it the first time). Update a favorite blog post and send it out again with additional information. If you're having a book signing, make sure the news gets sent out to your social media connections during peak times.

Peak Times for Social Media can be found by visiting this site: (socialmediatoday.com/brianna5mith/1453951/best-times-post-social-media-infographic)

If you offer contests or free merchandise, this is an added reason to return: I offer a free guide on getting published for a name and email address, and free stones with the purchase of "Conquering Your Goliaths: A Parable of the Five Stones." I then send interested parties (from my list) information on my new books, when I'm doing speaking events, book signings, etc.

Have any radio interviews? Get copies and post the links, short description and picture of the host on the first page of your website/blog, the higher up the page the better. This was a new addition to my website/blog in 2013. Check it out here: (www.ariverofstones.com).

Focus your blog: Don't make it about "anything" make it about "something" readers want. My blog focuses on writing, the techniques and skills as well how I've overcome many difficulties that a writer faces. Again, my website/blog can be found at: (www.ariverofstones.com).

Here Are a Few Blogs to Consider Writing For:

- **Kingdom Giggs** (www.kingdomiggs.com) accepts guest blogs and reviews you have written for other writers (another great way to promote)
- **Michael Haynes: A Writing Blog** (michael-haynes.blogspot.com)
- **MorgEn Bailey's Writing Blog** (www.morgenbailey.wordpress.com)
- **Mystery Writing Is Murder** (mysterywritingismurder.blogspot.com/)
- **Patricia Gilgor's Writers Forum** (pat-writersforum.blogspot.com/)
- **Printing By Design** with Ira Blacker (pbdink.com)
- **The View From My Window** with Diony George (www.diony-george.blogspot.com)
- **We Do Write** (we-do-write.blogspot.de)
- **Wise Words-Book Blogger** (www.louisewise.com)
- **Write Here, Write Now** with Sheila Boneham (sheilaboneham.blogspot.com/)
- **Writers and Authors** (www.writersandauthors.blogspot.com)

Interview on Your Blog:

Put out the word on your social media sites and your blog that you are interested in interviewing authors. When you get responses (and you will) attach a questionnaire to your email for the author to fill out and return to you.

Here is a list of questions I typically use for my interviews. Tweak and add as you wish.

1. Tell me a about yourself. What got you started in writing?

2. How and where do you write? Do you prefer a lap top or do you prefer writing freehand?

3. What's your favorite part about writing? Your least favorite part about writing?

4. How do you come up with your characters? Why would readers want to get to know them?

5. What types of marketing do you do to promote your writing?

6. How do you schedule your writing time? When do you write?

7. What are you currently working on? Do you have a new book out?

8. Do you have a project on the back burner? Tell me about it.

9. What would you tell a beginning writer who wants to publish but doesn't believe he/she has enough talent?

The important thing about interviews is to start with the easier questions, and work in the tougher ones at the end. No one wants to be put off by your first question they have no idea how to answer.

Also, try to keep your questions opened ended, meaning the writer must answer your questions with more than a 'yes' or a 'no.' I focus my questions on why writer's might write, how they write, what they are working on, and how they might help other writers get a head's up on writing.

Invite other Writers:

Round up some guest bloggers for your blog and watch the numbers to your site double or triple! The best news is that you'll make a new friend and you'll be able to give this friend free advertising, while, at the same time, increasing your readership.

Do a Blog Hop:

Blog hops are about getting the word out about your books with other writers who also blog and want to get the word out about their books. In this group setting you have the opportunity to help other writers as well as yourself through blog posts that promote your book where contests are usually initiated.

The **CIA Blog Hop** on Facebook is where I got started. This is a Christian Indie Authors closed group that works together on blog hops, so contact the site administrator to join in.

And lastly…

Consider what is happening in the real world: Ice-cream is really only as good as refrigeration. Leave it out for too long on the counter and it melts. Leave it too long in the freezer and it begins to grow crystals. Timing is everything when using real world events to spark up your author's blog/website.

Social Media Setup:

Is setting up your social media daunting? If you haven't yet connected with Twitter, Facebook, Linkedin and other important social media sites for authors or don't have time to set up an author page, get the help you need from Idea Creations Press. We will set up your social media for you, create your accounts and design your look. Contact us to begin the process.

Do You Write for Others?

- Writing for another's blog (writing a guest post) is a little like patting them on the back for doing such a great job on their site, and patting your own back in the process. They may not pay you in money, but they always pay you in free advertising. At the same time, you help grow their readership by the terrific blog post you've written.
- Blogs you have written for others will provide links to your books and website. If you do enough of these for others the results will come up on Google searches and you will be at the top of the list when folks want to learn more about you and your book.
- Blogs you have written for others will develop new friendships. When your next book comes out, the blog owner will more than likely want to publish something else you have written. In years to come, their blog readership will grow, and you can share your love of writing (or whatever topic you choose to write about) to even more followers, thus increasing who follows you on Twitter and Facebook.

Tips on Writing for Others:

- Offer a topic of interest. Read what is currently on their blog and offer something they'd be interested in.
- Keep to the rules. Write the length they want and include the links they want. If you're writing a piece to sell your work and it comes out as more advertising and less "I want to help

you with your blog" you'll usually find your work rejected by the blog owner.

- Thank the blog owner for posting your work, and work with them up until the time your work is posted. Make sure that you send your jpeg photo and book cover when they request it. Make sure your bio is short and to the point; many blog owners want the bio in third person.

- Don't be offended if the blog owner makes corrections or asks you to do so. The bigger the blog, in professionalism and readers, the more editing may be needed on your piece to reflect the style of the blog.

Some places I have written for:

- **Angela Parson Myers** (angelaparsonmyers.blogspot.com)
- **A Fiction Life** with Amber with Amber Stockton (amberstockton.blogspot.com)
- **Audrey Austin is calling all writers...** (writecreatively.blogspot.com/). Check out her website for authors who want to post a novel
- **The Book Connection** (www.thebookconnectionccm.blogspot.com)
- **Dee Doanes** (www.deedoanes.com)
- **eBookAnoid** (www.ebookanoid.com)
- **Elizabeth Spann Craig** (www.elizabethspanncraig.com)
- **Indie Tribe** with Charles Bray (www.theindietribe.wordpress.com)

Your Findings

Kathryn Elizabeth Jones

Your Findings

Social Media

We've already discussed how social media assists writers with other aspects of marketing, but the importance of social media in your book marketing plan bears repeating. Specifically, I use social media when:

- I've just published my book and want to tell my friends and readers about it.
- I want to share with them a segment of my book.
- I'm offering a free book as part of a contest.
- I'll be speaking at a particular event or with a group.
- I've just received my newest review or interview.
- I've just posted on my blog site or I've written for someone else and they've posted it on their site.
- I want to encourage other writers to continue.
- I want to share what someone else has written to inspire others to continue.
- I've come up with new options for readers such as an eBook or one-of-a-kind information presented from a YouTube video.

Social interaction doesn't have to be online, of course, but can be present at your favorite restaurant or gym (more about that later in the section, "Carry it with you"), but right now I want to focus on social media as it applies to promoting your book online.

Some Tips:

- Constant promotion can overload your readers. Make sure you are also writing blogs on your site and writing blogs for others that will help writers in their own writing.
- Make sure you respond to what your friends are saying. If they thank you for any reason, make sure you thank them back.
- Pay attention to what your friends are posting and reply to those things that strike you as interesting or profound. Others want to be noticed, too. Always include your website address so people can find you that want to connect.

Social media I use:

Facebook:

As an author you are going to want to create at least 2 pages, an author page and a book page. First, if you don't have a Facebook account, go to: www.facebook.com and create a personal account. Now, go to:
www.facebook.com/pages/create.php and follow the prompts to create your pages. A great resource for creating and managing your page is:
www.facebook.com/business/build.
Facebook has put together a vast help section to make your pages better.

In addition, the social media sites on Facebook are terrific for learning the ropes of writing, publishing and marketing, as well as getting the word out about your book. I use:

How to Make, Market and Sell Your Book -- All for Free, is an open group on Facebook specializing in authors helping authors to do the above three things. No promo of your own books is allowed here, but there is great opportunity to learn how to get the word out!

Another social media group on Facebook, **Writers to Encourage**, does just that; encourages writers in the avenues previously mentioned. Group is closed, meaning you'll need to contact the site administrator to join in. You can promote your work here, however.

Facebook Advertising:

Facebook is a great place to get some inexpensive marketing; market to specific areas of the world or country as well as various demographics. Check it out at:
www.facebook.com/advertising

Twitter:

Follow and be followed. Do you have gems to share? Share your blog here. Go to www.twitter.com to sign up. **Bitly** (www.bitly.com) shortens URLs that you use on Twitter. Say more because your URL has been shortened.

Twitterfeed:

Twitterfeed gets the word out automatically. Send your blog to Twitter, Facebook, Google, Linkedin and more without lifting a finger. Go to: www.twitterfeed.com to find out how.

LinkedIn:

Do you write fiction? Non-fiction? In either case, Linkedin is for you. Linkedin is a networking site for and about business people. Share what you do with editors, agents, bookstores and other writing related business connections. Create an account at: www.Linkedin.com.

LinkedIn also has some fascinating **social media groups** that will help you with your writing, publishing and marketing. Here are a few I like:

Market Your Book! is a great place to learn more about marketing. I am the site administrator. I also enjoy these groups: *Aspiring Writers; Authors & Writers of Fiction and Non-Fiction; Book Marketing; Christian Authors, Editors, Publishers and Bloggers; Book Publishing Professionals; Fiction Writers Guild,* and more...

LinkedIn Advertising:

Advertise your book to fellow business people. Advertise on LinkedIn at: www.Linkedin.com/ads/.

Pinterest:

Do you have a flair for the visual? Through Pinterest share your book through pictures, blogs you have written or the next place you will be signing. The possibilities are endless. You can set your account as an individual at: www.pinterest.com or as a business at: business.pinterest.com.

GoodReads:

GoodReads is a great site for people who love to read. Set up a personal account to share what you are reading and an author page to share your books. In addition, share about you, your blog, videos and upcoming events. Start at: www.goodreads.com.

Google +:

Create a Google+ account at: accounts.google.com. Google + is becoming increasingly popular and is a great way to link with others who enjoy what you do.

Google Advertising:

Create great inexpensive and focused advertising on Google. Go to: www.google.com/adwords.

Author Page on Amazon.com:

Go to: authorcentral.amazon.com to create your Amazon.com author page. Share all about you, your books, tour events, pictures, videos, blog and twitterfeed. Track your sales.

Yes, social media will take some time, so plan wisely. Then do some Google searching.

I find that once I've come across social media sites that I like, that I can return to find out the latest social media tactics. Rather than surfing the web for the next best article, I've found these sites to be invaluable:

http://www.inc.com
http://mattsouthern.com

http://www.socialmediaexaminer.com
http://bubblecow.co
http://ontext.com
http://www.ragan.com

You'll also want to try websites that offer free marketing material delivered to your email if you sign up on their site.

My favorite: www.PRWeb.com

In addition, it is always a good idea to find a writer friend who can help you with new social media ideas and vice versa. I often get some of my best ideas when I attend a writing class given by one of my writer friends.

Your Findings

Your Findings

Kathryn Elizabeth Jones

Your Findings

Word of Mouth

What you say about your book and how you say it has a bearing on who will listen, and ultimately, what will sell.

For example, say you're asked by a neighbor what your book is about and all you can tell him is a very rough idea of the plot. Or maybe you don't know what to say. You're stumped.

Ever heard of an elevator speech?

These speeches are long enough for the person to hear in an elevator between floors and are practiced at business meetings of all kinds throughout the world. In a good elevator speech, the person talks for 15-30 seconds about their product or service; what it is, what it does and why the person would want it.

A book elevator speech might go something like this:

"My book is about a woman by the name of Ms. Virginia Bean. One day she loses her job, a job she's held for many years. She decides to get a new job, and her first interview is with a man by the name of Mr. Spurt; only it's not really an interview that Ms. Bean is getting, but a meeting with God. She discovers the power of the five stones that God presents to her and uses them to get the job of her dreams."

This is my elevator speech, but it is not the blurb that's been written on my book's back cover. The elevator speech has to be more conversational; less rehearsed, and comes from your heart. Every time I give my elevator speech it's a little different, but the key elements as listed above, are there.

According to a recent Verso survey, 49.2% of readers "discover books" from personal recommendations, (no other pie piece is as large, including: bookstore staff recommendations and social networks!) That means that a personal, face to face chat is not only important, but invaluable to the success of your book.

So talk about it!

Your Findings

Your Findings

Kathryn Elizabeth Jones

Your Findings

Speak for Free

When I first began speaking for groups I wanted to get paid for what I did.

After all, hadn't I earned it?

The truth is, I hadn't earned anything, and people weren't going to pay me for what I'd written until they knew who I was, what I did, and why they should plunk their hard earned money on the table to receive what I had to offer them.

And so I began teaching free classes at conferences and my own free workshops. Sure, I was paid by some establishments, but my goal was to reach out to the community, share what was worthy of sharing, and allow those attending to receive what I had to give.

The money would come later.

Again, if your focus is on sharing what you have and helping someone else out, more than it is on making money on your speaking engagements or books, you will find that the right people will find you at just the right time and that the money will come when it is meant to come.

Ask yourself. What is my higher mission in writing this book? And make this higher mission your focus no matter where you go and no matter what you speak about.

Some Speaking Tips:

- Do what is comfortable in the beginning. If you stress out over PowerPoint, for example, make sure your first few classes are workshop oriented. Make up some worksheets to fill out as you speak. You may even find that your style doesn't lend itself to a PowerPoint presentation. My speeches usually don't.
- Have notes if you need them but don't read from a script. Ideally you want a presentation to go over seamlessly, with only key words written down as a guide. Look up often. Make eye contact.
- Give a short introduction of yourself, or have someone else do it for you; but make it short. People want to learn something to help them in their writing more than they want to know the life story of the speaker.
- Walk around. Try not to stand behind a podium unless you are doing a formal speech. Folks like to interact with the speaker rather than feeling separated from him/her.
- Use various elements of a good presentation; hands-on experiences, lecture, visuals, music…
- Save time for a question/answer segment. Fifteen minutes is good.

For Room Set-Up:

- Set up the chairs without an aisle down the center. Aisles tend to lose precious energy down the middle of the room instead of sending the energy out to the audience. If the chairs can't be moved and the aisle is standard fair, make sure as you speak that you travel from one side of the front to the other, thereby eliminating the lost energy, and making everyone in the audience feel that they are important no matter what side they are sitting on.

- Place the chairs close together with plenty of leg room. With the chairs close together, people have to talk to one another, (they are rubbing shoulders after all) with plenty of leg room, they have the space to visit.

- Make sure there is clearance on all sides of the room, so that wherever you walk you won't be tripping over cords or chairs.

- Use a microphone, especially if you're speaking in front of a larger group. A clip-on is nice because you don't have to worry about how close the mic is to your mouth or if you've remembered to bring it up to your lips.

- Place your books near the sign up table near the front of the room. You want the attendees to see your books as often as possible. You can also use the back of the room. Many presenters use the back and place a large sign or two in the area so folks know where they can purchase their books.

Getting Speaking Engagements:

Getting speaking engagements isn't always easy. And even if you get that speaking engagement, it isn't always easy to bring in the numbers. This is what I've done.

First, I piggyback with a well-known conference. For example, to get in to the last LDS Storymakers conference, I found out through a web search who was in charge. I emailed them, spelling out what classes I offered. They were interested in one of them and replied, stating that they could only pay a small honorarium but that I could sell my books. This conference caps at 400 attendees, so I knew the numbers would be there. The conference was well worth my time. I met some great people, sold some books, and even got away with my husband for a little honeymoon.

Second, I make sure that my website lists classes I offer and that my contact information is easy to find. I make sure that I spend time once a month searching for places to speak so that (if I'm not asked) my calendar is full for the year.

Third, I make up postcards to hand out where I can. I use these postcards all of the time. That means whenever there's even a slight chance of someone asking me to speak (even to a small group) I hand them a card. If I can get their information, even better. A follow up call or email will sometimes yield a speaking engagement.

Fourth, I speak to small groups like writers and readers book groups. You can always sell your books after your presentation or offer a special discount if they make a purchase before the event. It's usually better (especially with fiction) to have the group read your book before you come and speak; they will usually have more questions for you after the event.

Your Findings

Kathryn Elizabeth Jones

Your Findings

Offer Your Book for Free or Almost Free

There's nothing like get getting something wonderful to read for free! I like getting things free myself (with no strings attached, mind you).

Offering your book for free (for a limited time) will gather in new readers and maybe even some reviews, especially if you ask for them.

I offer my book free when:

1. It's recently been released.

2. Along with monthly celebrations like Black Friday or Christmas.

3. It's part of a blog contest.

4. When someone offers to review it.

***

Along with offering my book for free, I also advertise online as much as possible. Some outlets I have used:

Addicted to eBooks (www.addictedtoebooks.com/submission) offers free promotion for your eBook $5.99 or less.

Authors Free and .99 Promotional Book Club is a closed group on Facebook that allows you to advertise your free and .99 cent books.

Bookbub (www.bookbub.com) offers free promotion for your .99 cent book promo.

eFiction Finds (www.efictionfinds.com) is great for books priced $2.99 and under.

Free eBooks Reviews & Promotion (Join this social media group on Facebook)

Freebooksy (www.freebooksy.com)

Frugal Freebies (www.frugalfreebies.com)

Your Findings

Your Findings

Kathryn Elizabeth Jones

Your Findings

Get Some Free Advertising

Free advertising, are you kidding?

Nope.

There are blogs out there that will post your book, bio, video, first chapter and more...

Here are more than a few options:

- **Author Marketing Club** primarily helps with promotion ideas. A must read to learn more about advertising your book! (authormarketingclub.com/)
- **Awesome Gang** (www.awesomegang.com) displays an interview, bio, book cover and links. They will also announce your book on their Facebook page.
- **Black Caviar** (www.blackcaviar-bookclub.com) allows you to share your book blurb and links. Author interviews also provided.
- **Book Daily** (www.BookDaily.com) offers the writer the opportunity to display his/her book, bio, video and first chapter on their site.

- **Book Goodies** (www.bookgoodies.com) shows off your interview, guest post, author photo and links.
- **Book Grow** (bookgrow.com/feature-your-book/) will feature your book.
- **Book Hitch** (www.bookhitch.com) opens the way for you to share your book cover and links.
- To connect with **Book of the Day** on Facebook, contact (ebookpromoters@gmail.com). Send them information about your book. If they like what they see they will post it on their Facebook page.
- **Book Pinning** (www.bookpinning.com) allows you to pin your book cover on the site for free. Takes up to 24 hours to see your pin listed on site.
- **Pinterest** (http://www.pinterest.com) as mentioned previously, is another great visual outlet; it's been around longer, too.
- Jenai at **Bookingly Yours** (www.bookinglyyours.blogspot.com) will spotlight your book including an Amazon link, first chapter/excerpt and book cover.
- **Books Direct** (www.booksdirect.wordpress.com) provides a spot for your book cover, description, excerpt, book trailer, bio and review.
- Maurice at the **Bookshelf** (www.mauricetudorbookstore.wordpress.com) will display your author photo, book cover, bio and Amazon link.
- **Indie's Unlimited** (/www.indiesunlimited.com) will post a Sneak Peak of your book.
- Put together a puzzle of your book cover at **Jig Zone** (www.jigzone.com) and use it on your website or for social media promotion.

- **Make Mine Mystery** provides authors with free exposure; get your mystery excerpt, links, photo, bio and book cover on Morgan Mandel's site! (www.makeminemystery.blogspot.com)
- **New Book Blogger** (newbookblogger.blogspot.com/) offers writers, whether self published or traditionally published, to showcase their work.
- **Nothing Binding** (www.nothingbinding.com) shares your bio, author photo, video, book titles, descriptions and links. Also offers book reviews. Book Teaser only $5.
- **Polka Dot Banner** (www.polkadotbanner.com) allows you to post your profile, book cover and photos.
- **SPB roundup** (www.spbroundup.com/submit-info-about-your-spb-2) gives you an opportunity to post your book with links.
- **Sweetie's Pics!** (www.sweetiespicks.com/submit/) offers authors and other creative types to share their work. Post book synopsis, author photo, book cover, links and bio.
- **World Lit Cafe'** (www.worldlitcafe.com) posts your author bio, books, author photo and links. You can also be a reviewer.

Plug in "free book advertising" into your Google search engine and see what comes up. Also, remember that any blog post you write, any blog post you write for another site, and any time you talk up your book or share what you love with other writers—this is all free advertising.

Every few weeks I do a Google search on my books just to see what's out there and as long as someone isn't giving my books away for free (like a free PDF) without my knowledge, I feel pretty good about them sharing a book link from their site to Amazon, even if they haven't asked my permission in advance.

Your Findings

Kathryn Elizabeth Jones

Your Findings

Book Trailers

I don't know what it is about book trailers, but the thought of putting one together myself used to set me off. I couldn't afford to hire anyone, so I was stuck feeling pretty frustrated, that is, until I found **Animoto** (http://www.animoto.com).

Now, before you think that this section is merely an opportunity to spout off about one site, you're almost right, but you need to know I've tried other sites before I settled on Animoto. This is why I chose Animoto:

1. Animoto is easy. And I need *easy* straight out of the gate.

2. I didn't want to have to worry about copyright issues. All of the music I use, the photos (other than my own) and the short clips of media, have already been approved for use by Animoto.

3. It's easy to use my book cover as part of the video.

4. Book trailers are only 30 seconds. After that the minutes will cost me, so I always keep my trailers under half a minute. People have short attention spans anyway, so I am forced to focus on the message I want to convey.

5. After I've finished my book trailer I like that I can share it on Facebook, Twitter, Pinterest, Blogger, LinkedIn and more.

6. I usually export my video to YouTube and receive even more views.

I also use **Windows Live Movie Maker**. You can find free download instructions by Googling the title above.

I also like that fact that I can put together longer movies, use the company's effects, transitions, animations and themes, and that I can upload my movie onto Facebook and YouTube.

What I don't like is having to find music and pictures for my movie (that are not illegal for me to use) and this takes time. Still, I like the fact that if I want to put together a longer trailer, that I don't have to pay for the service.

The basics of putting a trailer together:

1. Make it short and memorable.

2. Use your book cover at least 3 times in the video.

3. Make sure you add your website/blog at the end of the trailer; mentioning it at least one other time is a good rule of thumb.

4. The music needs to fit your book. Check through the list before making a decision.

5. Make sure your sentences are short. Animoto doesn't give you loads of space for long-windedness; they limit your characters.

6. Most important, make it fun! What would you like to see in a trailer? What would you remember?

Your Findings

Kathryn Elizabeth Jones

Your Findings

Do Some Unheard of Book Signings

I'm not going to talk about the typical book signings here; most usually don't bring in too much traffic anyway. But if you do something different there is no end to your success. But you have to be willing to take a risk. Not all book signings will be what you expect, but there will always be an opportunity to meet new people, talk about your book and give away a free item so that those coming to your table will remember you.

Here are some ideas:
- Have a book signing at a grocery store, a garden center, a restaurant; somewhere that attracts a lot of traffic and that caters to your book. For example, one of my books has a sunflower on the cover for a reason; there is a point in the book where you'll read about sunflowers growing in a certain gentleman's front yard. One of my book signings is set up at a garden center near my home. What about a signing at a movie theatre, a pet shop, your local barbershop?
- Make your table attractive. Anyone can do a book signing with their books stacked on the table, but what if you brought in a table cloth, an easel to display one of your titles, some flowers, and some bagged stones with the words, Listening, Trust, Optimism, Tenacity and Constancy already labeled

and in a cellophane bag? (MY FREE GIFT).What if you also had postcards with your book on one side and a synopsis on the other? (Postcards will be talked about later).

- Stand up. Don't just sit behind the table, get up and talk to people as they walk by. Hand out your cards. Yes, this is a daring feat, but one worthy of you.

- Have a book drawing. Have a book reading. Do more than is expected of you. Have fun.

- Have a book signing at your home. Send out 200 invitations to friends, neighbors and acquaintances. Sign your books, do a reading; offer food or other activities to draw a crowd. For my book, "Scrambled," a cozy mystery, I invited friends and family to a scrambled egg breakfast at my home. For my book, "The Feast: A Parable of the Ring" I had a display of cupcakes. What do you think is on *this* book's front cover?

- At Christmas time (or other holiday times where people are shopping for gifts) have your book signing at a craft show. I did two of these shows during the Christmas season of 2012 and sold more books than I usually do at a typical book signing. I did one of the two mentioned craft signings the following year and did as well as I'd done the year before. Pay attention to the cost of the booth and the percentage you will have to pay organizers for your sales. I like to keep my booth price under $100; yes, there are some boutiques that demand $800 and up. (The most I have ever paid is 15 percent).

- Offer free items like bookmarks and trinkets (that represent your book) before your speaking event. Or get there early and hand out postcards with your contact information on them.

- Remember, book signings can (and should be) held following every speaking engagement, even when you speak to a small writer's group.

Kathryn Elizabeth Jones

Your Findings

Carry it with You

One of the most rewarding experiences I have had in selling my book is carrying my book with me.

A couple of year ago I was at a conference. The woman sitting next to me asked what I did for a living. I told her. Yes, I gave her my elevator pitch with a few variables. I handed her a postcard. She thanked me. The conference went on. When I stood to go home she stopped me.

"I would like your book," she said.

I took the book out of my purse, she paid me the money, and I autographed the copy for her.

That simple.

Some writers carry a box of books in the trunk of their car, or a couple of copies in the glove box. But it's the same concept. Carry your book with you because you never know when the book will come at the right time and place for someone else.

Kathryn Elizabeth Jones

Your Findings

Offer a Free E-book or Paperback Copy in a Contest

Sure, you can send a paperback copy off to the winner, but you can also offer an eBook. There are many blogs out there that offer contests, though they may not review your book. Some of the ones I've used:

- **Cozy Mystery Book Reviews** (cozymysterybookreviews.com/)
- **I Am a Reader Not a Writer** (www.iamareader.com)
- **Keeping Up with the Rheinlander's** (www.mnmrheinlander.com/)
- **Make Mine Mystery** (www.makeminemystery.blogspot.com)
- **Pondering by Andrea** (andrealschultz.blogspot.com/)
- **Spunky Seniors** (spunkyseniors.blogspot.com/)
- **Wall-to-Wall Books** (wall-to-wall-books.blogspot.com/)

Even if you offer a print copy as your winning book (something that will cost you a little bit of money), consider this: All the exposure you'll receive!

Offer a Contest on Your Site:

It's easy to put together a drawing for your new book. One of my favorite ways to get other readers and authors interested in winning is to ask them to post an answer to a question related to the book, share their own writing experience, or come up with their own idea.

On one such contest I had readers share their favorite Halloween idea. I chose my favorite entry. At other times, just sending your name and email will get you entered into the contest.

I haven't used Rafflecopter (www.rafflecopter.com/rafl/instructions/) yet but installing it on your computer is free of charge and enables you to keep track of the entries you've received.

When I've entered contests using Rafflecopter, I am often able to enter multiple times by following the instructions provided.

Your Findings

Kathryn Elizabeth Jones

Your Findings

Use Postcards instead of Business Cards to Promote Your Work

Give out postcards as free gifts. Yes, postcards will cost you but you can get them pretty cheap. You'll need book cards to hand out at book signings, when you're eating at a restaurant, when you're talking to someone about your book.

On one side of the card is your book cover, on the other, the synopsis, contact information and QR Code. What is a QR Code? Here's mine. If you take a picture of my QR Code using your Smartphone, you'll be able to go to my website directly from your phone!

I've also considered getting my QR Code printed on the back of some T-shirts. Imagine people coming up to you (or whoever else is wearing your shirt) and taking a picture of your QR Code.

Here's where I've used my cards:

- Given to a manager at a restaurant, thanking him for the great service (and, yes, it was great).
- At various stores. Sometimes I ask the manager if I can leave a few on the table or near the store's entrance, at other times I just leave them on countertops and tables.
- Bulletin boards at grocery stores are great.
- I have handed them out at business meetings (the social networking kind).
- I have taken them to church.
- I have used them at speaking engagements and book signings.
- I give them away as a book mark when someone buys one of my books.
- I take them with me everywhere. The cards are in a sealable bag in my purse to keep from getting crushed.

Marketing your book takes time so expect to work hard, especially in the beginning when you are learning the ropes. It's been said that writing a book is difficult, but marketing is the hard part that comes after that.

Here's hoping that many of my ideas have cleared the road a bit.

Happy Marketing!

Kathryn

Your Findings

Kathryn Elizabeth Jones

Your Findings

P.S. Now that you've finished this book, expect FREE yearly updates in PDF format via email by providing me with your email address.

Contact me at: kathy@ariverofstones.com to request your FREE yearly PDF copy!

Kathryn Elizabeth Jones

Idea Creations Press

Remember the swings as a kid? Remember how the wind felt against your cheek and the freedom you experienced? We want you to feel just like a kid at Idea Creations Press, and we expect that you'll be in wondering awe your entire swing.

And why not?

We know you have some GREAT IDEAS that you'd like turned into a book, and our writing services give you that one-on-one time you need and expect, whether it's through phone connection, email or personal visit. Get your book ghostwritten, or have an expert editor give you suggestions on your finished book for improvement. We respect your ideas, and always place them in the #1 position.

This is YOUR project. And that makes you the first and the last word.

Idea Creations Press is a publishing services company utilizing Print on Demand (POD) technology; hence, you own the rights to your work. That means you decide how you want to market and sell your books. And you make the profit.

At Idea Creations Press we know you've worked hard on your book and want to PUBLISH IT without waiting years to see it in print. We also know you need help MARKETING what you've published or are soon to publish. Standard publishing is difficult to find these days, even for an exceptional book, so why not get your work out there easily? Why not get the marketing you need to sell your book without spending a royal mint?

From Idea to Creation, let Idea Creations Press sit you on that glorious swing of success!

Rest assured we're here to give you that never-to-be-forgotten dream experience.

So, what are you waiting for?

Idea Creations Press

Here is a list of our services.

Writing Services
Ghostwriting
Blog Writing
Classes &Workshops
1-Article Mentoring
2-Children's Picture Book Writing & Mentoring
3-Children's Book Writing & Mentoring

4-Novel Writing & Mentoring 101

Editing
Editorial Evaluation
Basic Copyediting
Comprehensive Copyediting

Layout & Design
Custom Full Color Book Cover
Custom Book Cover Illustration & Design
Professional Book Cover Photography * Design
Black & White Interior Illustrations
Color Interior Illustrations
Professional Interior Photography
Custom Interior Formatting
Ultra Custom Interior Formatting
Designer Book Interior
Image Insertions
Barcode
ISBN Assignment
e-Book Creation & Distribution
Standard Press Release
Press Release Distribution
Library of Congress Catalog Number Assignment
U.S Registered Copyright
QR Codes

Publishing Options
Standard Book Publishing
Expanded Book Publishing
Full-Color Book Publishing

Marketing
Personal Marketing Assistant
Marketing Telephone Consultation
Book Review Submission
Author Social Media Set-up

Other Items Available
Business Cards
Postcards
Bookmarks
Banners & Stands
Sell Sheets
Posters
Custom T-Shirt featuring your Book

authorsupport@ideacreationspress.com
http://www.ideacreationspress.com
http://twitter.com/kakido
http://www.facebook.com/IdeaCreationsPress

Your Findings

Kathryn Elizabeth Jones

Your Findings

Made in the USA
San Bernardino, CA
28 January 2014